I0436614

BILLY M. MORENO

How to Invest In Real Estate

Proven Strategies for Real Estate Hidden Profits

Copyright © 2024 by Billy M. Moreno

All rights reserved. No part of this publication may be reproduced, stored or transmitted in any form or by any means, electronic, mechanical, photocopying, recording, scanning, or otherwise without written permission from the publisher. It is illegal to copy this book, post it to a website, or distribute it by any other means without permission.

Billy M. Moreno asserts the moral right to be identified as the author of this work.

First edition

This book was professionally typeset on Reedsy.
Find out more at reedsy.com

Contents

Introduction

Sarah stared at the eviction notice, a cold pit gnawing at her stomach. She was single and had a lot of debt, so the thought of losing her small apartment made her feel like she was being thrown into a cold sea. Just then, a worn-out paperback fell off her shelf from a spot she hadn't looked in a while. In the dim light, "Investing in Real Estate: Proven Strategies for Hidden Profits" shone. Even though Sarah wasn't sure about the book, she read it all in three sleepless nights. After a few weeks, she wasn't freezing in the street; she was hammering nails into a fixer-upper that she bought with money she got from the book. The renovation was hard, but Sarah turned the eyesore into a cozy haven with the help of do-it-yourself tips and her increased confidence. Within months, she rented it out for a lot of money, which not only paid for her own housing but also gave her a steady stream of income. Sarah's life, which had been empty before, was now full of possibilities thanks to the book that helped her find the hidden potential in real estate. At first, she thought it was just a desperate dream.

Do you remember Sarah? Her story isn't an anomaly. It's the spark that ignited this book, proof that real estate holds secret profits waiting to be unearthed. This isn't just a guide to buying and selling; it's a treasure map leading to financial freedom, passive income, and a future filled with possibilities. Whether you're a seasoned investor or a novice like

Sarah, these pages hold the keys to unlock hidden wealth within the concrete jungle. Forget conventional advice; we'll dive deep into niche markets, creative financing tricks, and strategies that turn fixer-uppers into gold mines. You'll learn to master the market, build your dream team, and manage the legal and tax waters with confidence. Ready to ditch the eviction letters and start writing your own success story? Then step into the vibrant world of real estate, led by the secrets these pages hold. Forget spreadsheets and jargon; this is an adventure packed with actionable strategies and real-life examples that will empower you to change your financial landscape, one hidden profit at a time.

Unveiling the Hidden Profits of Real Estate

Understanding the power of leverage and appreciation

Picture yourself with a heap of vibrant balloons during a carnival. You want these balloons to keep floating higher and higher because they represent your money, right? Similar to a massive helium tank is leverage. It provides you with a large burst of air to expand your balloons even further! Rather than using your own money to purchase a single balloon, you borrow it from the tank (a mortgage lender) and purchase several. Your balloons are now rising, but there's a catch: you have to return the borrowed air later, along with interest. The trick, though, is that you can sell your balloons for even more money than you borrowed if they grow in value. This profit represents the strength of leverage, even after the debt has been repaid. Visualize a fixer-upper home. You purchase it with leverage, perhaps investing as little as 10% of your own funds. After making minor repairs and adding some shine to your balloons, it sells for a lot more than you originally spent. The distinction—boom, undiscovered profit! Like the sun rising, appreciation will gently raise your balloons even higher. Real estate, including land and homes, tends to appreciate in value over time for the following reasons:

- **Growing population:** As more people require housing, demand and costs will rise.
- **Economic development:** Businesses and jobs are drawn to thriving towns and cities, which raises the value of real estate.
- **Restricted supply:** Since there is a finite amount of land and it cannot be expanded, current properties are becoming increasingly rare and precious.

Thus, you can blow up your financial balloons by combining the helium blast of leverage with the gentle lift of appreciation! Recall that there are hazards as well. You can owe more money than your assets are worth if the market declines and your balloons burst. Thus, it's imperative that you:

- **Make an investigation:** Recognize the property and market you are investing in.
- Invest sensibly by selecting homes with strong appreciation potential.
- Take control of your debt by not taking on more than you can afford.

Unlocking the hidden benefits of real estate through appreciation and leverage may be an exciting journey to financial freedom with smart planning and a little amount of risk!

Exploring diverse income streams beyond rent

Get rid of the stale cliché of the landlord tallying piles of cash from rent receipts. While a reliable rental income is essential to real estate investing, the most astute participants understand that the real riches is found in diversifying their sources of income. Consider your property to be a treasure box full with undiscovered hidden riches!

Consider these fascinating revenue streams and think beyond the box of rent:

Holiday Leasing

Make a carefully considered property, or your second home, into a weekend sanctuary. Through websites like VRBO and Airbnb, you can meet interested travelers looking for unusual experiences. Picture quaint cabins tucked away in the forest, sunny beachside bungalows, or hip downtown lofts brimming with urban vitality. Every vacation opens up an additional revenue source on top of your usual tenant.

Solutions for Storage

Do you have any empty space? Make it into gold! Secure storage spaces can be rented out, including spare closets, garages, and attics. Enthusiasts, downsizers, and students are constantly searching for secure places to store their possessions. You may turn square footage that you might not even be utilizing into a reliable source of income with little financial outlay.

Co-working Areas

The shift to remote work has made it possible to turn empty commercial facilities into vibrant co-working spaces. Provide conference spaces, high-speed internet, and flexible desk rentals to fulfill the demands of independent contractors, business owners, and remote employees. Community and convenience are the lifeblood of this revenue stream, benefiting both you and your enterprising tenants.

Services and Facilities Offsite

Provide useful on-site services to enhance the value of your property and go beyond just charging rent. Bike rentals, pet grooming salons, laundry facilities, and even automobile charging stations can draw customers and bring in extra money. Recall that contented tenants are devoted tenants, and these facilities improve their quality of life, which helps you in the long run.

Hosting an Event

Do you have a large backyard or a pretty rooftop patio? Make it a place for events! Organize small weddings, pop-up markets, birthday celebrations, and yoga retreats. Your property can earn a solid dose of event-day revenue by becoming a sought-after venue for special occasions with a little marketing and inventiveness.

Dispelling common myths and misconceptions

Discovering a worn-out map that seemed to hold the secret to hidden wealth. However, there are numerous signs along the route alerting people of "**bottomless quicksand**" and "**cursed krakens**." These, my friend, are fallacies and myths surrounding real estate that are meant to frighten you away from the true wealth that lies beneath the surface. With the knowledge and proven tactics found in this book, we will be equipped to traverse these murky myths and uncover real estate's hidden gains. We're going to clear the air and clear your way to financial freedom, so buckle up!

Myth # 1: You need a wad of cash the size of Scrooge McDuck.

Nope! There are inventive financial techniques like "house hacking," in which you live rent-free as your mortgage is paid for by your property. Imagine enjoying a cup of coffee in your home while knowing it's discreetly increasing your fortune. Not too terrible, huh?

Myth #2: It's all about reality TV drama and house flipping.

Fixer-uppers may be thrilling, but there are many other kinds of real estate wealth. Consider stable rental income from flats, adventurous people's vacation rentals, or even storage units for people collecting childhood mementos (guilty!). Everybody can find the ideal "hidden profit" niche.

Myth #3: Dreams are devoured by the market, a terrifying beast.

Although the market does fluctuate, information is still power! We'll discover how to identify the most promising prospects by using our investigative skills to data analysis, demographic comprehension, and trend analysis. Knowing the beast's movements will help you not to be afraid of it.

Myth #4: You must have a Wall Street swagger and an expensive outfit.

Everyone can own real estate, whether they are a shy bookworm or an outgoing social butterfly. All you need is a little perseverance and the appropriate equipment. This book will be your real estate equivalent of a Rosetta Stone; it will help you quickly decipher the code and feel like an accomplished agent.

So, adventurer, set aside the myths and get your map! This book holds the secret to uncovering the hidden rewards that await you in real estate. One brick at a time, let's turn myths into mileposts and pave your path to financial free.

Defining Your Investment Goals and Risk Tolerance

Assessing your financial standing and future aspirations

Embarking on an exciting journey in the realm of real estate investment is really wonderful. Let's take a moment to assess your ship's seaworthiness, or more specifically, your financial stability, before you hoist the anchor. Why? Because, like any journey, a lucrative and seamless one requires an understanding of one's limitations and goals. Let's start by spreading out our financial map, which includes bank statements, income, and debts. We'll need to know what kind of treasure chest you have to start, whether it be stable income, debt, or savings. This makes it easier for you to determine how much you can commit without feeling like you're in uncharted territory. Let's dream a little now! Imagine yourself where you want to end up—financially independent, retiring early, or creating a rental empire. Which way of living are you yearning for? At what income level would you consider yourself to have struck gold? Your compass, which directs you toward the best financial options, is these objectives. Recall that your ability to tolerate risk is what will keep you afloat in the turbulent waters of the market. On a scale of "cautious captain" to "high-seas daredevil," rate your own personality. Do you like possible windfalls and fixer-uppers, or are you content with gradual and consistent revenue streams? By selecting investments that fit your comfort level, you can avoid those bothersome financial krakens by being aware of your risk tolerance. You are going to put yourself in a successful position by making this crucial initial move. You'll be aware of your financial situation, your goals, and the level of risk you're willing to accept. Now take out your financial map, draw a route to your ideal location, and let's embark on this real estate journey together! Recall that a well-planned trip equals success, and with these resources at your disposal, you're set to sail the high seas—er, the real estate market, that is!

Identifying investment horizons and return expectations

Setting out on any real estate journey requires knowing where you're going. This covers not only the amount of earnings you hope to make but also the time frame you anticipate reaching it. To put it simply, we must determine your investment horizon and match it to your anticipated rate of return.

- **Investment Horizon:** Think of this as the length of time you plan to hold onto your property. Do you want to flip your house quickly—within a year? Are you imagining an empire of long-term rentals? Or is it in the middle of your sweet spot? Your choice of tactics will depend on how well you understand your horizon.
- **Expectations for Returns:** This is the point at which you picture your treasure chest brimming. Do you give renting first priority when it comes to income flow? Are you planning to sell for a tidy profit and are seeking capital appreciation over time? Or is your ideal situation a combination of long-term growth and income? To maximize success, make sure your expectations are in line with the horizon you have selected.

- **The Intertwined Dance:** It is essential to comprehend how these two elements interact. Strategies such as flipping fixers, which yield quick returns but may entail greater risk and work, are frequently preferred by investors with short time horizons. Long-term perspectives, on the other hand, provide slower but possibly more reliable returns through value-driven investments or steady rental income streams.
- **Discovering Your Harmony:** Your own situation and objectives will determine the "perfect" balance. A young professional with a high threshold for risk may decide to go for a high-potential, short-term flip. On the other hand, a family getting ready for retirement would place more value on steady, long-term rental income.
- **The Takeaway:** This isn't a one-size-fits-all recipe. You will have the knowledge and skills necessary to evaluate your individual circumstances, determine your level of risk tolerance, and specify your time horizon for investing and expected rate of return. Keep in mind that these are flexible and can change as your circumstances and objectives do.

You may map a clear path to real estate wealth by lining up these essential components. Your return expectations serve as the compass that directs you, and your investing horizon acts as the wind in your sails. With each voyage, the hidden profits of real estate will draw you nearer if you navigate strategically.

Mapping out your risk tolerance and comfort level

Consider investing in real estate as a flavorful, yet hot, dish. Although the pleasures are tantalizing, one mishandled bite could give you heartburn. This is where risk tolerance comes into play; it's the ability to withstand a certain amount of heat before becoming uncomfortable.

It's important to map this out before making any hasty property acquisitions. So tell me, how do you gauge your "spice-o-meter?". It involves having an open discussion with oneself and posing inquiries such as:

- **Big aspirations vs. steady drip:** Do I want to rent out my property quickly and at a high risk, or slowly and steadily?
- **Rollercoaster or soft sway:** Can I ride the waves with some composure, or does the prospect of market changes send chills down my spine?
- **Sleep tight or toss and turn:** Would a possible decline in my property's value keep me awake at night, or could I weather the storm without having any restless nights?

The responses to these inquiries provide a topography of your risk tolerance. Perhaps you're an experienced mountain climber, at ease with sheer drops and sheer cliff faces. Alternatively, you can be a beach bum who enjoys the soft tide's ebb and flow. There is a real estate plan out there that is ideal for you, regardless of your style. *Recall that being knowledgeable is more important than being fearless.* With the information and resources in this book, you will be able to evaluate your comfort zone, investigate various investing possibilities, and identify the ideal balance between possible gains and restful sleep. Take a deep breath, identify your unique comfort zone, and get ready to prepare a tasty dish of financial success that is spiced with just the appropriate amount of risk before diving into the exciting world of real estate. This is something you can handle!

Mastering the Market Analysis Arsenal

Demystifying market cycles and identifying trends

Have you ever had the impression that cryptic cycles and complicated language envelop real estate markets? As if you need a crystal ball to see into the future? Adventurer, unwind! We'll provide you the skills in this chapter to help you deconstruct market cycles and spot trends like a pro investigator. You only need basic investigative sense and a few useful tools—a crystal ball is not necessary. Think of the market like a huge swing set. There are moments when it's skyrocketing, with happy "woohoos" as prices rise. At other times, it falls, leaving folks with empty pockets and somewhat green faces. Selecting the ideal moment to purchase, sell, or just hang on tight requires an understanding of these cycles, which include booms, busts, and everything in between. However, how can you recognize these tendencies before they slam into you? Don't worry, data—numbers that convey tales about the market— is our first hint. Consider rental costs, vacancy rates, and even area demographics and job growth. You'll notice patterns emerging, akin to a sly cat peering out from behind the curtain, as you learn to read these numbers. Next, watch the wider picture, including changes in the economy, national trends, and even the Fed's occasional cranky tweet. Even though you may not be familiar with all the technical terms, knowing the broad direction of these pressures might help you anticipate potential effects on your neighborhood swing set. Lastly, keep in mind that patterns are subject to change. Their guidance is like to that of wind whispers; it does not possess authority over you. Utilize your enhanced ability to understand markets to make well-informed judgments that suit your objectives and comfort level. Avoid being deterred by apprehensions about a downturn or becoming easily distracted by exaggerated claims during periods of market excess. Equipped with your data detective kit, broad perspective, and a healthy dose of prudence, you'll be able to confidently traverse the market and identify patterns and cycles before the general public does. Recall that being knowledgeable about the market is about making informed decisions in the here and now, one methodical step at a time, that will lead to real estate success rather than trying to forecast the future. Ready to unlock the market code? Set aside the crystal ball and grab your magnifying glass! A hidden profit treasure box is waiting for you!

Evaluating local demographics and economic forces

Real estate investing is a purposeful endeavor that requires a keen understanding of market trends rather than being a random lottery. And what more useful instruments are there than studying the economic and demographic dynamics that determine its very existence? Envision a bustling metropolis. Millennials moving in droves to a hip neighborhood? The market for chic studio flats there is really promising. An aging population looking for comfortable bungalows? It's time to think about single-family houses in quiet suburban areas. It is easier to identify the kinds of homes that will appeal to prospective tenants or buyers when one is aware of the area's income distribution, age distribution, and lifestyle trends. But think about the city's economic engine as well; it's not only about the people. Is it a thriving IT center with plenty of well-paying jobs? or a vacation hotspot drawing sporadic tourists? Rental rates and property values are directly impacted by these factors. Now, try not to be put off by the technical terms. We're not talking about manipulating intricate spreadsheets or reading official reports. This book will provide you with easily accessible web resources and useful advice to:

- **Discover changes in the population's makeup:** Use interactive maps and census data to monitor changes in family income, the age distribution, and population growth.
- **Gauge economic health:** Analyze job markets, unemployment rates, and important industries to get a sense of the community's financial health.
- **Find rising stars:** You may find hidden treasures in areas that are seeing infrastructure development, neighborhood revival, or thriving business districts.

Through the integration of demographic and economic factors, a comprehensive understanding of the market's future potential can be obtained. You'll be able to predict demand, spot underutilized markets, and eventually make well-informed investment choices that eliminate chance. Thus, keep this in mind the next time you hear rumors about market trends: you're not a lost lamb in a complicated maze. Equipped with the skills and information in this book, you will become an expert navigator, skillfully navigating the terrain of economic and demographic forces and prepared to identify the most favorable conditions for your real estate aspirations to materialize.

Evaluating local demographics and economic forces

Although the real estate market is full of opportunities, figuring out its subtleties can be like trying to solve an old puzzle. Invest with courage and fear not! With the help of this toolkit for market analysis, you may break through the barriers and understand the secret language of economic and demographic forces. Consider a flourishing city as a dynamic ecosystem. Studying its population's ages, income brackets, and habits is similar to researching the local flora and wildlife. Modern flats are popular with young professionals, and pensioners prefer quiet surroundings. Once these patterns are understood, it becomes possible to determine which kinds of homes will succeed in each area. But that's not where the narrative ends. The real estate landscape is shaped by economic forces, much as an ecosystem is maintained by sunlight and rainfall. Is the city a hotspot for tech, drawing in big salaries? A paradise for tourists full of transients? These elements affect property values and rental rates, functioning as the market's weather patterns. But do not panic! This book helps you become an expert economic signal decoder by providing you with easily accessible web resources and useful advice.

- **Unmasking Demographic Shifts:** Use interactive maps and census data to monitor population growth, age distribution, and income levels. Imagine yourself working as a cartographer, illustrating the future demographic geography of the market.
- **Taking the Heartbeat of the Economy:** Examine job markets, unemployment rates, and important industries to gauge the local economy's health. You'll develop into a proficient diagnostician who can spot regions with robust economies and appealing investment prospects.
- **Finding Rising Stars:** Keep an eye out for areas experiencing infrastructure development, commercial district growth, or neigh-

borhood rehabilitation. These are your prospective gold mines, the places where the seeds of your investments can grow into big profits.

You become a self-assured navigator by learning the languages of economic and demographic forces, rather than just a confused traveler. You'll eliminate chance from the equation by predicting demand, spotting underutilized markets, and making wise investment decisions. This book is your Rosetta Stone, giving you the ability to decipher the market's complexity and turn them into understandable and useful insights. Now enter the busy real estate market, learn to understand its complex language, and find the way to success in your investments.

Utilizing data analytics and property search tools

Data and effective search tools are the key to the future of real estate analysis, so forget about crystal balls and tea leaves. These aren't only for Wall Street whizzes; you can have them in your arsenal and use them to fight an exciting war for lucrative investments. Consider data to be the market's whispers, revealing unseen patterns and profitable prospects. This book will teach you to listen intently, and you may use user-friendly platforms and internet tools to:

- **Follow real estate trends:** With interactive graphs and heatmaps, you can see past price shifts, pinpoint area hotspots, and even forecast future prices. You don't need a statistics degree or a calculator!
- **Find hidden gems:** Look past the standard postings to find homes off the beaten track. Strong filters might highlight good deals that aren't often seen, fixer-uppers that could use some work, or rental homes that are ready to move into.

- **Compare and conquer:** To choose the property that stands out from the competition, consider factors such as rental rates, competitiveness, and local amenities. Think of it as an apples-to-apples comparison on steroids!

However, data is only the starting point; the true power is unleashed when it's combined with advanced search technologies. Envision a digital genie fulfilling all of your requests related to real estate! You may even search houses with specific remodeling permits or rental history by using filters that include phrases like "pet-friendly" or "rooftop terrace" and setting financial limits. It's similar to having a private tour guide for the whole real estate market in the city. Recall that becoming a master analyst does not require a degree in data science. This book gives you the confidence and abilities to successfully traverse the world of online tools and data by breaking down difficult ideas into manageable, practical steps. What's the best thing, then? These resources democratize the power of knowledge and provide you with an advantage in the cutthroat real estate market because they are frequently free or easily accessible. Prepare to unleash the power of data and search tools, then polish your digital sword. By turning the murmurs of the market into audible cues that point you in the direction of your ideal investment, this book will serve as your Rosetta Stone. Keep in mind that information is power, and you're well-equipped for success in the data-driven real estate industry.

House Hacking: Living Rent-Free While Building Wealth

Implementing the BRRRR strategy: Buy, Rehab, Rent, Refinance, Repeat

Put an end to landlord stress and rent checks! The ability to live rent-free while accumulating real estate riches is made possible via house hacking. The secret? The BRRRR approach, a potent acronym that stands for

- **Buy:** Identify a property with potential, preferably below market value and in a desirable location. Imagine unpolished diamonds rather than glistening castles.
- **Rehab:** A comprehensive makeover is not necessary; even cosmetic changes can make a big difference in value.
- **Rent:** Get dependable tenants who will pay your mortgage each month and enjoy your freshly renovated home. Consider stable income rather than eviction letters.
- **Refinance:** Take advantage of the equity in the property by doing a cash-out refinance when its value has grown as a result of your upgrades and dependable tenants. With this magic trick, you'll get your money back plus some extra to put toward your next trip.

- **Repeat:** Rinse and repeat! Now that your wallets are full, go out there and take down another fixer-upper, one rent-free sanctuary at a time, expanding your real estate empire.

The BRRRR method is not a piece of cake; it takes preparation, diligence, and a little bit of elbow grease. However, there is no denying the benefits for those prepared to put in the work:

- **Bid farewell to rent:** picture yourself living in a home of your own, unencumbered by the capricious demands of landlords or soaring rental costs. Hello, financial freedom!
- **Passive revenue streams:** Each tenant turns into a tiny money-maker that helps you stretch your budget by adding to your monthly income.
- **Equity growth:** Your property portfolio and net worth increase with each profitable BRRRR cycle, laying the groundwork for long-term financial stability.

Optimizing rental income and property value

House hacking offers a steady, calculated route to real estate wealth; forget about "Get Rich Quick" gimmicks. Imagine having multiple units and not having to pay rent as your renters pay down your mortgage and increase your equity. Seems too wonderful to be true? Rethink your thoughts. The goal of house hacking is to maximize rental income and property value rather than just cutting down on rent. The two main components of this magic trick are:

Careful Leasing:

- **Recognize your worth:** Set competitive yet lucrative rentals for your units by examining rental rates of nearby properties that are similar to yours.
- **Choose the appropriate tenants to target:** Draw dependable tenants with a track record of timely payments who respect the property. Use internet resources and a thorough screening process to choose tenants quickly.
- **Think beyond rent:** Explore alternative income streams like laundry facilities, storage spaces, or even parking spots. Little things build up over time.

Enhancing Value Upgrades:

- **Put your attention on wise upgrades:** Give projects that increase resale value and tenant satisfaction top priority. Consider energy-efficient fixtures, modern appliances, or freshly painted walls.
- **Curb appeal matters:** Spruce up the exterior with landscaping, lighting, or a fresh coat of paint. In the process of drawing in tenants and possible buyers, first impressions matter.
- **Don't overrenovate:** Stay away from pricey modifications that might not be appealing to a wider market and stick to changes that are useful and have a good return on investment.

Navigating legal and tax implications

Picture yourself enjoying the life of luxury, rent-free, in a home that you own, with money from another portion of the property miraculously covering the mortgage. This is the magic of house hacking, my friends—a tactic that works just as well as it sounds. But let's talk about the big picture first: the legal and tax ramifications, before you jump headfirst into this financial freedom paradise. Do not be alarmed, brave home invaders! It is not necessary to be a licensed accountant or have a law degree to navigate these waters. This book will serve as your reliable compass, providing you with helpful advice and concise explanations of the most important financial and legal ramifications of house hacking.

Let's start by discussing legality:

- **Zoning Laws:** Verify that the house hack you have in mind complies with zoning laws that permit the occupancy of many units. Any questions can be answered by having a polite conversation with the local zoning department.
- **Lease Agreements:** Create comprehensive lease agreements that clearly define the obligations and regulations surrounding tenancy for your tenants. It is usually a good idea to get a brief assessment from a lawyer.
- **Insurance:** Verify that your policy covers your particular scenario of being hacked into from home. We may need to upgrade to a landlord policy.

And now for the fascinating realm of taxes:

- **Deductions:** If you hack a house, you can write off costs like as property taxes, mortgage interest, and depreciation on the portion that is used for rental income. Wonderful tax reductions!
- **Income Reporting:** Although rent must be reported as income, you don't need to worry about it because the amount that you deducted will balance the taxable amount.
- **Capital Gains Tax:** Keep in mind that you can only deduct capital gains taxes from the sale of the property on the portion that you

used as your primary residence.

It's crucial to remember that laws and tax consequences can change based on where you live. This book will give you a broad overview; but, for more specific counsel, it is always advisable to speak with a local tax expert or attorney. Recall that while house hacking is an effective tactic, it's important to take legal and tax implications into account. You can fully utilize this rent-free wealth-building technique and manage these aspects with confidence if you arm yourself with knowledge and seek professional help when necessary. Now, inhale deeply, gather your compass, and let's go on this journey of house hacking together! This is something you can handle!

Flipping Fixers: Unveiling Untapped Potential

Identifying bargain properties with hidden renovation potential

Some people view fixer-uppers as intimidating eyesores and potential money pits. However, astute investors see it as a hidden treasure, a diamond just ready to be polished into a profitable gem. Finding cheap houses with unrealized remodeling potential is crucial. Consider it similar to treasure hunting. Forget gold doubloons; your prize lies hidden under overgrown gardens, creaking floorboards, and layers of peeling paint. This part will provide you the map and compass you need to find your way through these murky waters and find the rough gems that could end up becoming your crown jewels in real estate.

Above and Beyond Bargain Basements

Don't merely go for the cheapest item. Seek for properties in prime areas with strong bones. A well-built home in a growing neighborhood may need some cosmetic work, but the return on investment could be substantial due to its intrinsic value.

- **Friend rather than enemy:** Accept the surface imperfections. Do the bathroom tiles have cracks? dripping faucet? Frequently, these are resolvable problems rather than catastrophic ones. Don't let them deter you from a home with a fantastic layout, roomy interiors, or attractive architectural features.
- **Plan Ahead, See Possibilities:** Imagine the finished item. Is it possible to turn that messy garden into a calm haven? Is it possible to open up the kitchen and make a contemporary living area? You can evaluate the actual potential and decide whether the renovation expenses are worthwhile by visualizing the "after" image.
- **Undiscovered Treasures:** Don't pass on off-market prospects. Before they make their way onto the glossy open house circuit, diamonds can be found through bank foreclosures, expired listings, or even word-of-mouth rumors. Take the initiative, make connections with locals, and keep an eye out for

Estimating renovation costs and timelines

Turning a rough diamond into a brilliant gem is the key to flipping houses successfully. However, it's imperative that you become skilled at projecting restoration costs and schedules before picking up a paintbrush and sledgehammer. Consider it like creating a treasure map: discovering hidden earnings might become a tedious treasure hunt in the absence of precise locations. So, how can we make sure our renovation budget doesn't resemble a runaway balloon and steer clear of expensive surprises? This book will serve as your reliable guide as it will lead you through the following:

- **Exposing the Hidden Costs:** Renovation estimates are constructed brick by brick, not in one piece. Divide the project into manageable chunks to begin with. This can include plumbing, electrical, flooring, roofing, and so forth. Look up the typical prices in your area for each component, taking into account things like labor rates and material selections. Always provide for unanticipated events by allocating a contingency buffer (10–15%) to account for gremlins that could be hiding in the walls.

- **Making Friends with the Contractor Compass:** On this journey, don't undertake it alone! Get estimates from many trustworthy contractors that are experts in the kind of work you need done. Be explicit about your expectations, timeframe, and budget. Request a breakdown of their estimates, taking into account labor expenses, where to get materials, and any necessary permits. Examine comparable projects side by side to see which contractor best balances value and quality.
- **Time travel for profit:** In the quick-paced business of flipping, time truly is money. Precisely projecting the duration of your remodeling guarantees that delays won't sap your profits. Divide the project into manageable stages, accounting for reasonable times for demolition, building, inspections, and finishing. To prevent unpleasant timeline shocks, make sure you and your contractor are in agreement on expectations and keep a regular check on progress.

Maximizing resale value and profit margins

Imagine a buried diamond that has been neglected and covered in dust, waiting to be found and polished. In the real estate market, these "diamonds in the rough" are frequently properties that need work and have unrealized potential. The real excitement of real estate investing comes in flipping these diamonds, maximizing their resale value and making a tidy return. However, remodeling fixer-uppers is not a random magic trick. It's a calculated dance, striking a balance between astute remodeling and acute market insight. You will learn how to waltz with both in this book, turning those dusty diamonds into shimmering gems.

Increasing the Resale Value

- **Recognize your audience:** Examine regional market patterns to determine what consumers want. Is it the quaint old touches or the slick, modern finishes? Adjust your renovations based on what the market wants.
- **Put "high impact, low cost" first:** Take on important aesthetic upgrades like new paint, modern fixtures, and practical floor plans. Give priority to areas where improvements have the most return on investment, such as bathrooms and kitchens.
- **Avoid over-renovating:** Fight the want to turn your community into a golden palace in a bronze one. Investing excessively in opulent finishes may reduce your profit margins.

Increasing Profitability

- **Budget like a hawk:** Carefully estimate renovation expenditures, taking unanticipated expenses into consideration. Never forget that in the flipping world, surprises almost never bring good news.
- **Haggle like an expert:** Develop your negotiating abilities when purchasing the property and obtaining supplies. Your bottom line benefits from every dollar saved.
- **Money is time.** Establish and adhere to a reasonable renovation schedule. Like a leaking faucet, delays can eat away at your revenues.

Through careful application of these techniques, fixer-uppers can be turned from cheaply made diamonds to highly desirable properties that will yield the highest possible returns for you. Recall that flipping involves more than just hammers and paintbrushes—it also requires market knowledge and strategic decision-making.This book will act as your guide, taking you through every stage of the flipping process, from identifying potential that has been buried to optimizing profit margins and resale value. Put on your strategic toolset, put on your metaphorical hard hat, and be ready to be amazed by the jewels hiding inside those fixer-uppers. The dazzling benefits of a profitable flip are in store!

Creative Financing: Beyond the Traditional Mortgage

Harnessing the power of seller financing and hard money loans

This chapter opens the doors to a secret world of creative financing, where aspirations dance with unique funding strategies. Forget the stiff boundaries of typical mortgages. Put an end to feeling limited by traditional loans; in this place, we'll unlock the potential of hard money and seller finance to support your real estate goals.

Seller Finance: A Friendly Handshake with Opportunity

Imagine negotiating directly with the landowner and eschewing the banks completely. A new option is made possible by seller financing, in which the seller serves as your lender and distributes payments over a certain time and interest rate. It's based on mutual trust and benefit, much like a handshake deal. This strategy is quite effective for:

- **Increasing your purchasing power:** You can acquire your ideal home before traditional means ever come into play by avoiding large down payments.

- **Reaching a flexible agreement:** Adjust the terms of repayment to your cash flow to reduce your financial stress and give yourself some breathing room.
- **Developing connections:** Building a strong relationship with the seller might lead to future business prospects and market knowledge.

But keep in mind that a solid grasp is necessary for every handshake. With the guidance of this book, you will be able to confidently negotiate seller financing agreements that benefit both sides.

Hard Money Loans: Quick Cash for Astute Traders

Time is money, and traditional loans might occasionally seem to move slowly. Let me introduce you to hard money loans, the thrill-seekers of the finance industry. For time-sensitive transactions or fixer-upper properties in need of urgent upgrades, these private lenders provide speedy access to funds, frequently within days. But just like a rollercoaster, making hard money has its ups and downs.

- **Higher interest rates:** In comparison to standard mortgages, be ready for higher expenses. These are not long-term mortgages; rather, they are intended for short-term projects.
- **More stringent qualifications:** Lenders place a premium on project potential and property value, requiring thorough documentation and well-thought-out exit tactics.

Invest with courage and fear not! With the information and resources in this book, you'll be able to successfully negotiate the fast-moving world of hard money loans and receive the money you require without becoming sidetracked by potential dangers. Recall that creative finance is a strong weapon that should be used with wisdom and caution rather than like a magic wand. This chapter will help you understand seller financing and hard money loans so you can take advantage of their potential and use them to finance your real estate endeavors beyond what regular lending can offer. Watch your real estate ideas take off when you leave the bank and enter the exciting realm of creative finance!

Exploring private lending options and joint ventures

To be honest, conventional mortgages sometimes seem like a solitary, rickety bridge leading to the world of real estate investing. However, what if we told you that there is a network of undiscovered routes, such as joint ventures and private finance, just waiting to carry you, much more easily and adaptably, to your real estate objectives?

Private Lending

Think of it as your own personal financial fairy godmother. Put an end to your piles of paperwork and rigorous bank procedures. Private lenders are people or businesses looking for alternative investments, and they can provide custom loans with conditions that meet your requirements. Want a higher APR loan with a shorter term? Perhaps a flexible timeframe for repayment? Often, private lenders can help these aspirations come true. But wait, not every fairy godmother is dressed in a beautiful gown. Extensive research is essential. With this book assistance, you will be able to:

- **Recognize reliable lenders:** Acquire the skills necessary to recognize reliable partners and proceed confidently in the world of private loans.
- **Negotiate like an expert:** Develop your ability to close deals to

get the greatest conditions and interest rates, making sure your financial magic carpet isn't full of unstated costs.

- **Organize the transaction for success:** Recognize the many kinds of private loans (bridging, hard money, etc.) and select the one that best suits your investment approach.

Joint Ventures

Envision a group of treasure seekers combining their resources and knowledge to find a buried wealth. That's what joint ventures are all about: working together with other investors to split the expenses, risks, and gains of a real estate project. Through this partnership, doors that might otherwise be unopen are opened. Imagine collaborating with someone who has the money to buy a sizable building even though you don't. That ideal home suddenly becomes a real possibility. This novel will

- **Assist you in finding the ideal companion:** Recognize the various kinds of joint ventures and find investors who align with your objectives and skill set.
- **Create a win-win contract:** Discover how to set up a joint venture such that there are clear lines of accountability, equitable profit sharing, and a seamless exit plan.
- **Handle conflict and communication:** Give yourself the tools and techniques to handle disagreement so that your treasure quest stays productive and friendly.

Through the process of demystifying joint ventures and private lending, this book turns into your key to unlocking secret routes to real estate success. You won't be constrained by the rickety old bridge of conventional funding any more. Thus, embrace the unorthodox, investigate these alternate options, and observe as your financial horizons grow beyond what the bank can offer. The road to real estate wealth is paved with opportunity for flexibility, teamwork, and perhaps even a more comfortable journey.

Structuring deals for optimal profitability

Do you believe conventional mortgages are the only way to get access to real estate? Rethink that! This chapter goes beyond the traditional and explores the world of creative financing, where transactions are designed to maximize your profit and reveal opportunities that were previously undiscovered. Put an end to strict loan applications and exorbitant down payments. An array of choices is presented by creative financing, each providing a distinct route to property ownership and wealth generation. Consider:

- **Seller financing:** Seller financing entails collaborating with the seller and accepting lease-to-own or progressive payments. Building trust and possibly obtaining a reduced purchasing price is similar to shaking hands.
- **Hard money loans:** These quick-term private loans fill the gap between what you can afford and the home of your dreams. Consider them as stopgap measures that open the door for more conventional funding in the future.
- **Collaborative projects:** Join forces with other like-minded investors to combine resources and purchase larger, more promising properties. Imagine splitting the costs and rewards while constructing a real estate empire piece by piece.

However, how these arrangements are structured isn't up for grabs. Negotiation skill and meticulous planning are necessary for maximum profitability. We'll give you the resources to:

- **Consider each option:** To select the financing that best fits your needs and budget, consider factors including interest rates, payback schedules, and associated hazards.
- **Haggle like an expert:** Develop your ability to communicate effectively and discover how to create agreements that are advantageous to both parties.
- **Defend your interests:** Recognize the legal ramifications and protect your investment by using clear contracts and agreements.

Beyond Single-Family: Demystifying Niche Investments

Exploring opportunities in vacation rentals, student housing, and storage units

Although single-family homes are the traditional real estate investment vehicle, there is a rich universe of niche options available to the daring (and astute) investor. Let's explore hidden gems like holiday rentals, student housing, and storage units instead of making generic decisions. These places provide distinct difficulties and equally unique rewards.

Profits From Sun-Kissed Vacation Rentals

Envision relaxed families having fun in your personal pool, tucked away in a picture-perfect seaside community. Both visitors and investors can experience a little piece of paradise with vacation rentals. Peak season rental rates combined with the possibility of longer stays might result in large profits. But keep in mind that overseeing vacation rentals calls for a keen sense of hospitality and the ability to predict what visitors would want. With the help of this book, you'll be able to manage reservations, handle busy times of year, and provide unique experiences that entice customers to return.

Living & Learning: Hostels for Students

Campus communities teem with youthful vitality, and their demand for student housing provides a consistent flow of occupants. Imagine having a steady stream of revenue from rentals from apartments close to busy campuses, where value is paramount and accessibility is key. Nonetheless, meeting students' specific wants and preferences calls for an awareness of them. Consider social areas, lease flexibility, and accessibility to campus centers. This book will walk you through navigating student restrictions, taking advantage of this dynamic market, and designing living spaces that support both community spirit and academic performance.

Everything Has Its Place: Storage Units

Storage units are more than just ancient artifacts in our society that is always growing. They provide a profitable niche for investors and are havens for valuables. They are the epitome of passive income due to their minimal upkeep and steady rental revenue. However, don't undervalue the game's strategic aspects. It's critical to comprehend the tenant's requirements, security features, and location. This book will reveal the inner workings of this sometimes ignored industry, showing you how to get the most out of your storage unit investment and maximize its functioning.

Understanding the unique challenges and rewards of each niche

Discard the notion that single-family dwellings are the only type of real estate. The world of investing is full with uncharted territory that await the daring investor to discover and conquer. Dwelling in these niches can reveal unique obstacles and even more unusual rewards. Examples of these niches include sun-drenched vacation rentals and storage units brimming with forgotten treasures. But thorough research is necessary before venturing into unknown territory. This book will provide you the information to traverse each niche's terrain, grasping its unique benefits and possible hazards, much like any intrepid traveler requires a map:

- **Vacation Rentals:** Picture sunny beaches and secluded mountain retreats that can bring in a steady stream of revenue. It sounds wonderful, doesn't it? But keep in mind that accommodating transient visitors and handling seasonal openings need for adaptability and a flair for hosting.
- **student housing:** Being close to colleges ensures consistent rental income, but be ready to navigate student-specific rules and deal with late-night pizza parties.
- **Storage unit:** These little spaces are always in demand and require little upkeep, even though their facades may not be particularly appealing. On the other hand, controlling access and handling misplaced items can be an unforeseen challenge.

Diversifying your portfolio for resilience and growth

Even though single-family houses are the stereotypical representation of real estate, there is much more to the investment landscape than well-kept lawns and white picket fences. Investing in niche markets, which are sometimes disregarded despite their immense potential, can be your hidden weapon in the real estate game, boosting growth and resilience. Imagine your portfolio as a thriving garden. No matter how lovely they may be, planting simply sunflowers leaves you open to seasonal variations. However, by adding a variety of plants, such as fragrant herbs and robust cactus, you may build an environment that is resilient and thrives all year round. Similar to your exotic orchids and climbing vines, niche investments give your real estate portfolio depth and flexibility. Think about these exceptional opportunities:

- **Vacation Rentals:** Envision shady mountain cottages and beaches bathed in sunlight. These sources of income-producing refuges satisfy short-term demand and provide a nice change of pace from conventional long-term leases.
- **Student housing:** Colleges develop vibrant communities around co-living and microapartment spaces. These high-demand, low-maintenance solutions can attract younger, tech-savvy tenants and provide consistent rental income.
- **Storage Units:** The demand for safe storage is increased by the advent of urban life and minimalist fashions. Purchasing climate-controlled real estate offers low vacancy rates and steady revenue streams.

Diversification has real advantages:

- **Protecting against market swings:** Diverse markets respond to changes in the economy in different ways. A decline in one industry could be countered by a surge in demand in another, keeping your total returns stable.
- **Finding hidden treasures:** Because there is less competition and unmet demand in niche areas, prospective returns are frequently larger.
- **Spreading your risk:** You reduce the impact of unanticipated occurrences on any one asset by investing in a variety of property kinds and locations.

Assembling Your Dream Team: Realtors, Contractors, and Property Managers

Finding trustworthy and competent professionals

No one has established an empire on their own. And when it comes to real estate, your search for undiscovered wealth necessitates a formidable dream team consisting of astute brokers, knowledgeable contractors, and trustworthy property managers. However, it might be intimidating to navigate the professional jungle. How can you find reliable partners who support your achievement and share your vision?

Locating Your Dream Home, Robin:

- **Look for local knowledge:** Seek out seasoned real estate agents with a strong presence in the market you are targeting. Their understanding of local customs, laws, and trends is priceless.
- **Transcend credentials:** While impressive resumes are wonderful, real passion and effective communication are priceless. A realtor who shares your enthusiasm and comprehends your objectives is invaluable.
- **Follow your instincts:** Set up interviews, pose insightful questions, and pay attention to your gut. Select a person who gives

you confidence and with whom you can establish a solid working rapport.

Revealing the Conquistador of Construction:

- **The most important factor is reputation:** Look for contractors who have a track record of doing high-quality work, finishing projects on schedule and within budget, and leaving happy clients. Look over their internet reviews and request references.
- **Specialization counts:** Match your investment goal with your contractor's area of expertise. Experts in renovation are necessary for flipping fixer-uppers, but maintenance experts are needed for managing rental homes.
- **Openness is essential:** Make sure there is clear deadlines, thorough bidding, and open communication. Select a contractor who values your confidence above everything else and responds to concerns promptly.

Recruiting the Paladin of Property Management:

- **Experience is the shield:** Seek managers with a strong understanding of tenant dynamics, rental regulations, and efficient property maintenance strategies.
- **Use technology to your advantage:** Seek out managers who use it to automate processes, improve communication, and offer owners and tenants easy-to-use online portals.
- **A human touch:** Look for someone with outstanding people skills who is skilled at resolving problems with tenants and building strong bonds. Recall that contented tenants result in greater occupancy rates and reduced stress levels for you.

By thoroughly screening your ideal team, you create a foundation of competency and trust that allows you to concentrate on the larger picture—uncovering the hidden earnings in your real estate ventures. Keep in mind that your team is a reflection of you, so make good decisions and foster a strong sense of teamwork. Together, you will conquer obstacles, negotiate the complexities of the market, and turn your goals into a prosperous real estate empire.

Defining roles and responsibilities

Picture a symphonic orchestra. Each unique but essential instrument contributing to the harmonic creation of a masterwork. A well-assembled team, with each member providing their specialized knowledge to ensure the success of your investment, is also necessary for your real estate journey. This group, your ideal team, is the secret to overcoming the difficulties involved in purchasing, maintaining, and eventually achieving financial independence with real estate. But assigning roles and tasks is essential to the success of your team, just as an orchestra cannot play without a conductor. Now let's examine the key players and their distinct roles:

The Lead: Your Real Estate Agent

Consider your realtor to be the conductor, skillfully leading your investing goals into action. They are adept in negotiating contracts and navigating the ups and downs of the market to help you land the property of your dreams. Their duties include:

- **Identifying suitable properties:** coordinating the potential of the place and market trends with your investing ambitions.
- **Encouraging seamless transactions:** From the first discussions

to the last paperwork, they guarantee a smooth and stress-free transaction.

- **Getting around local regulations:** They are experts at zoning rules, permits, and legal nuances, which makes property ownership simple.

The Constructors: Your Associates

Your contractors convert potential into profit, much like the construction team brings designs to reality. They carefully handle repairs and restorations, acting as the architects of your vision:

- **Project cost estimation:** They offer precise quotations and transparently monitor budgets, covering both labor and supplies.
- **Performing high-quality work:** They place a premium on quality and adherence to building codes, whether they are performing simple maintenance or a major overhaul.
- **Communicating effectively:** Open communication throughout the project keeps you informed and ensures your vision translates into reality.

Your property managers are the caregivers.

Your property managers look after the daily upkeep of your investments, much like the committed stagehands do:

- **Letting and tenant screening:** They locate dependable renters, take care of papers, and oversee leases.
- **Rent collection and financial reporting:** Maintaining your cash flow rhythm requires prompt rent collection and clear financial

reporting.

- **Property upkeep and repairs:** Proactively preserving the property's value by attending to tenant problems as soon as they arise.

Recall that your ideal squad is dynamic. It may grow to include marketing experts, tax experts, and legal counsel based on your investing goals and portfolio size. Finding the precise roles and duties that meet your goals is crucial to ensure that everyone contributes to making your real estate journey cohesive. You will use this book as a guide to put together your ideal team. We'll go more deeply into each member's area of expertise while offering helpful advice on selecting qualified experts and promoting productive dialogue. Recall that an efficiently managed team is an investment in your success, advancing your real estate goals with each harmonious note of cooperation. So get your musicians together, decide on their tunes, and be ready to see your investment symphony come to a grand finale. With a dream team on your side, your real estate empire awaits, one harmonious note at a time.

Fostering effective communication and collaboration

Putting together your ideal real estate team requires more than just locating qualified experts—it also requires establishing a foundation of cooperation and efficient communication. Imagine it as building a skyscraper, with a property manager overseeing smooth operations, a builder erecting the robust frame, and a realtor laying the groundwork. Even the most talented people can leave you with an unstable tower that is susceptible to unforeseen gusts of wind if there is a lack of effective communication and coordination. So how can you foster this foundation of cooperation? The following are some crucial tactics:

- **Establish Clear Expectations:** Identify duties and responsibilities right away. Be open and honest about your objectives, preferred methods of communication, and methods of reaching decisions. This helps to prevent confusion and annoyance in the future.
- **Open Communication Channels:** Promote an environment where people communicate honestly and openly. Promote frequent updates—both good and bad—and provide channels for helpful criticism. Keep in mind that, when faced cooperatively, even obstacles can present chances for development.
- **Make Use of Technology:** To improve communication and project management, embrace internet resources and tools. Apps for communication, document repositories, and shared calendars can help to streamline procedures and keep everyone in the loop.
- **Celebrate Successes:** Acknowledging and applauding accomplishments, no matter how minor, boosts confidence and team spirit. A quick "thank you" or a group lunch can make a big difference in creating a supportive and cooperative atmosphere.
- **Proactive Problem-Solving:** Problems will inevitably come up. Treat them as group problems rather than personal vendettas. Collaboratively generate potential solutions by utilizing one another's skills and viewpoints to arrive at the best possible answer.

You can turn your dream team from a group of people into a cohesive entity that works for your real estate objectives by fostering these communication and teamwork techniques. Keep in mind that while a house may be constructed using bricks and mortar, a real estate empire that lasts is based on enduring bonds and a spirit of cooperation.

Mastering Landlord Zen: Efficient Property Management Strategies

Screening tenants and navigating the legal landscape

The delicate art of Landlord Zen, a state of attentive management where effective tenant screening and legal knowledge assure harmony in your property portfolio, is just as important to real estate success as bricks and mortar. Proactive tenant selection and familiarity with the legal environment are essential components of effective property management, much like meticulous weeding and tending to a tranquil garden.

Tenant Selection: Fostering Harmony:

- **Adopt a detailed approach:** Reference checks, credit reports, and background checks are more than simply formalities; they're your insurance against future administrative and financial difficulties.
- **Seek alignment, not perfection:** Get along with your tenants before looking for the "perfect" tenant. Seek out accountable people whose requirements and standards coincide with your property and management approach.
- **Pay attention to your gut:** Put your intuition before papers. Don't

disregard warning signs during interviews or discrepancies in your application. Going cautiously can help avoid problems down the road.

Getting Around the Legal Maze:

- **Accept cooperation over antagonism:** Recognize that tenant rights and fair housing legislation exist for the mutual protection of both parties. Reducing legal risks can be achieved in large part by forming a transparent and respectful cooperation with your tenants.
- **Preventative actions are essential:** A clear framework for resolving any potential conflicts is created by precisely worded lease agreements, comprehensive move-in/move-out procedures, and constant documenting of communication and repairs.
- **Seek expert advice:** See knowledgeable property management specialists or legal counsel whenever in question. Their knowledge may guide you through tricky legal issues and help you steer clear of expensive blunders.

Recall that thorough tenant screening and legal knowledge are routes to peace of mind, not only instruments for averting issues. By making these upfront investments, you create an environment of accountability and trust that frees you up to concentrate on the real return on your investment—a healthy rental portfolio that provides you with both peace of mind and stability in your finances as you pursue your real estate goals.

Maintaining and enhancing property value

Finding quiet tenants and being paid on time aren't the only things Landlord Zen does. It's about accepting the responsibility of being a steward of property worth and working hard to preserve and grow the financial potential of your investment. Consider it similar to growing a bonsai tree: careful maintenance guarantees not just long-term health and value but also aesthetic beauty. So, how does one become a property value zen master? The following are some fundamental ideas:

- **Your mantra should be preventive maintenance:** Plan checks on a regular basis, take quick action when wear and tear occurs, and give preventative maintenance priority over expensive repairs down the road. Recall that if tiny leaks are not addressed, they can grow into massive waterfalls.
- **Modernize with a Mindful Eye:** Take into account deliberate improvements that raise the usability and appeal of the property. Modern fixtures, energy-efficient appliances, and technological integrations can draw in better renters and enhance property values.
- **Curb Appeal Promotes Cash Flow:** A well-kept façade has a lot of influence. Well-maintained pathways, new paint, and lush landscaping make a good first impression, which increases rental prices and speeds up the tenant acquisition process.
- **Adopt Sustainable Solutions:** Take into account environmentally beneficial modifications like solar panels or water-saving fixtures. They not only lower operational expenses but also draw in tenants that care about the environment and follow expanding market trends.
- **Take Careful Notes, Make a Decision:** Keep thorough records of all repairs, invoices, and correspondence with tenants. This

safeguards your legal interests and gives you useful information for future budgeting and strategic planning.

Recall that optimizing your long-term return on investment is more important than focusing only on aesthetics when preserving and increasing the value of your house. Adopting these tactics and taking a thoughtful, proactive approach to property management will help you create a thriving asset that will withstand market swings and appreciate in value over time.

Building positive relationships with tenants

It takes finesse to negotiate the landlord-tenant relationship. You are, on the one hand, a conscientious business owner protecting your capital. Conversely, you are cultivating an environment in which individuals flourish. The secret to mastering this dance and reaching Landlord Zen is cultivating a good rapport with your tenants. Consider your home as a small community as well as an investment. Tenants are your inhabitants, and investing in their well-being is not just a thoughtful gift but a calculated risk that will pay off in the long run and bring you peace of mind. The following are some guidelines for developing peaceful relationships:

- **Communication is Key:** Create early on lines of communication that are open and transparent. Respond to their questions promptly, make yourself available, and actively hear their concerns. Recall that they are people, not merely renters, who should be treated with dignity and compassion.
- **Transparency is a Virtue:** Be clear about expectations, maintenance schedules, and rent. Share necessary papers, reply to requests for information immediately, and eliminate hidden costs or surprise

expenses. Transparency eases conflict and fosters confidence.

- **It's Important to Perform Timely Maintenance:** Avoid letting a dripping faucet turn into a furious melody. Assure fast and effective repairs, be proactive in addressing possible problems, and swiftly respond to maintenance requests. Tenant churn is decreased and appreciation is fostered by a well-maintained property.

- **Treat Your Tenants as Partners:** Keep in mind that the health of the property is a shared interest between you both. Promote responsible conduct, provide justifiable modifications when possible, and cooperate to find a win-win solution to problems. Working together promotes mutual respect and lessens conflict.

- **Go Above and Beyond:** Little things have a big impact. Keep birthdays in mind, send greetings for the holidays, or provide new renters with a welcome box. These small gestures not only make a good impression, but they also set you apart from the "landlord by the numbers."

Being kind isn't enough to create a healthy relationship; you also need to understand how your success is correlated with others' success. Tenants that are content are more likely to maintain the property, pay their rent on schedule, and stay. Ultimately, you're investing in your own financial security, peace of mind, and a healthy real estate portfolio when you make an investment in their well-being.

Navigating Taxes and Legal Considerations

Understanding tax implications of different investment strategies

Even the most seasoned investor can get chills just thinking about taxes. But in the dynamic world of real estate, knowing the tax ramifications isn't about avoiding dragons; rather, it's about arming yourself with knowledge so you can confidently traverse the intricate terrain. You already have the tools in this book to expand your business, find hidden earnings, and cultivate tenant relationships that are zen-like. Let's now provide you the skills you need to handle the tax side of things and make sure your success is both legally compliant and financially safe. Consider various investing approaches as routes out of this tax tangle. Every one has its own turns and turns, its own unspoken clues and possible dangers. Here's a peek at how to handle the tax ramifications of certain important tactics:

- **Fixer-upper flips:** It can be thrilling to make rapid money on a successful flip, but keep in mind that Uncle Sam is entitled to his part. Recognize depreciation deductions, capital gains taxes, and the possible effects of holding periods. With the knowledge in this book, you'll be able to maximize your earnings once the tax man bites.

- **Renting for Reliable revenue:** While creating a consistent flow of rental revenue is a wise move, it is taxed income. Find information about depreciation, repairs, and property management charge deductions. Make the most out of your tax plan to retain more of your hard-earned rental money coming in.

- **Investigating specialty Opportunities:** Every specialty, from storage units to holiday rentals, has particular tax issues. You will learn about particular deductions, depreciation schedules, and possible tax advantages related to various types of property from this book. Understanding the tax environment in your selected specialization will keep you informed and financially safe because knowledge is power.

Taxes are just a part of the journey, not something to be feared or avoided. While this book won't instantly turn you into a tax accountant, it will provide you with the fundamental information and tools you need to make wise choices and, when necessary, seek professional advice. You can guarantee the legal and sustainable growth of your real estate business by being aware of the tax ramifications of your investment strategy.

Protecting your assets with insurance and risk management

Real estate ownership is thrilling, but remember that there is huge potential and great responsibility. Like medieval knights defending their castles, we contemporary real estate tycoons need to outfit our empires with risk management and insurance. Consider insurance as your dependable protection, preventing unanticipated blows from accidents involving renters, property damage, and even legal problems. Selecting the appropriate policies, from liability coverage to fire and flood protection, is like fortifying your stronghold with the best weaponry. But keep in mind that insurance has its limitations, much like any protection. This is where risk management enters the picture, your crafty plan to reduce weak points and avoid conflicts entirely. Here's how to construct your unassailable stronghold:

Essentials of Insurance

- **Property Insurance:** Shield your property from fire, storm, and other physical damage. Don't cut corners on insurance; a poorly covered castle quickly comes apart.
- **Liability insurance:** Defend yourself against lawsuits stemming from accidents or destruction of property on your property. Although accidents may occur, your liability insurance can protect you from financial hardship.
- **Tenant Insurance:** To reduce your risk to possible tenant accidents, encourage tenants to get their own policy. Remember that shared responsibility is the lifeblood of a well-guarded castle.

Expertise in Risk Management

- **Comprehensive Upkeep:** Examine your property on a regular basis and take quick action to solve any potential risks. A well-kept castle is impervious to intrusions from broken wiring and leaking roofing.
- **Lease agreements and screening:** Thoroughly vet potential tenants, spell out expectations in lease agreements, and keep meticulous records of everything. An alert commander keeps intruders from breaking through your gates.
- **Safety precautions:** Implement safety protocols, such as smoke

detectors and fire extinguishers. Taking every safety measure fortifies your defenses against unanticipated threats.

Your real estate empire becomes nearly impenetrable when you combine the proactive risk management techniques with the protective shield of insurance. Recall that preparedness is essential. By foreseeing possible dangers and implementing preventative actions, you reduce the likelihood of harm and guarantee that your assets are adequately safeguarded throughout time. Hence, don't let a fictitious sense of security deceive you. Invest in the appropriate insurance, develop your risk management abilities, and observe as your real estate empire soars under the watchful eyes of readiness and safety. And never forget that sage counsel can be of assistance to even the most powerful strongholds. Seek advice from licensed insurance agents and attorneys to customize your defenses to your unique situation and create a long-lasting stronghold.

Staying compliant with regulations and legal frameworks

The combination of the terms "legal" and "taxes" doesn't exactly make most people tingle with joy. To ensure smooth sailing and prevent mistakes, it is imperative to comprehend and navigate these issues in the dynamic realm of real estate. But don't worry, you can overcome this terrain without a machete and an Indiana Jones cap. We will provide you with clear guidance and measures to demystify the legislation and legal frameworks.

Making a Tax Map Chart

- **Recognize the different tax types:** Recognize taxes on rental income, depreciation, and capital gains. Look into any credits and deductions you might be eligible for. Consult a tax expert; they will explain the terminology and assist you in making the most out of your tax planning.
- **Maintain accurate records:** Track your expenses, income, and property upgrades. Well-maintained records make tax filing easier and help avert audits. Consider it as creating a well-defined route through the tax maze.
- **Keep abreast of any changes:** Just as butterflies migrate, so do tax laws. To stay up to date on updates that could affect your real estate assets, subscribe to pertinent periodicals or speak with a tax professional.

Constructing a Stronghold of Law

- **Become familiar with tenant-landlord laws:** Understand your legal obligations and rights with regard to leases, tenant rights, and evictions. Being ignorant is not bliss; by following the law, you and your tenants are protected.
- **Protect your assets:** To safeguard yourself against unanticipated circumstances, think about getting property, liability, and title insurance. Consider it as erecting a strong, compliant wall around your investment.
- **Seek expert advice as necessary:** It is advisable to leave complex legal concerns to experienced professionals, such as property disputes or contract discussions. Seeking legal advice from a real estate lawyer or attorney is similar to bringing in an experienced jungle guide when things become complicated.

Recall that adhering to laws and rules doesn't have to be a difficult or lonely endeavor. Through proactive action, knowledge acquisition, and professional help when necessary, you can confidently navigate the terrain and ensure that your real estate endeavors grow alongside thriving legal and tax clarity.

Extra Advice: Adopt technology! Numerous internet tools and sites help handle legal documents, track deductions, and make tax calculations easier. It can be even easier to navigate the jungle with these digital machetes.

Conclusion

Best wishes! You've traveled through the unexplored areas of this book, through the intricate world of investing methods, and discovered the hidden treasures in the real estate industry. Now, take a proud stance at the edge of your abilities, prepared to plant the seeds that will grow into a flourishing business of your own creation. But keep in mind that temporary fixes and fads don't create success. It is nourished, grown, and cared for with steadfast commitment and tactical foresight. This book has served as your seed packet, providing the information and resources you need to plant your ambitions in fruitful soil. It's up to you, my friend, to handle the rest. Allow changes in the market to act as a mild wind to fortify your financial foundation. And never lose sight of the ultimate prize: security, independence, and a legacy that you personally and cleverly constructed brick by brick. This book is a beginning, not an end. With the skills you've acquired, the tactics you've refined, and the self-assurance you've built, enter the dynamic real estate market with unflinching determination. Recall that good fortune rewards the brave, the knowledgeable, and the tenacious. Venture forth, explorer, and tend to the kingdom that lies in wait inside the concrete jungle. The seeds of success have already been sown; allow your ambition to be the light that nurtures them into a resilient forest. Thus, put this book to bed with a shout of excitement rather than a sigh of accomplishment. Your real estate aspirations are only ahead of you, lighted by your newly acquired knowledge and paved with possibility. Step one, step two, and watch your empire grow, brick by brick, into a monument to your drive and the wealth of undiscovered potential within.

www.ingramcontent.com/pod-product-compliance
Lightning Source LLC
Chambersburg PA
CBHW071159290526
45796CB00007B/80